John Dee: The Life and Legacy of the English Occultist, A Philosopher Who Became Queen Elizabeth I's Spiritual Advisor

By Charles River Editors

A late 16th century portrait of Dee

About Charles River Editors

Charles River Editors provides superior editing and original writing services across the digital publishing industry, with the expertise to create digital content for publishers across a vast range of subject matter. In addition to providing original digital content for third party publishers, we also republish civilization's greatest literary works, bringing them to new generations of readers via ebooks.

Sign up here to receive updates about free books as we publish them, and visit Our Kindle Author Page to browse today's free promotions and our most recently published Kindle titles.

Introduction

A contemporary engraving of Dee

"Who does not understand should either learn, or be silent." – John Dee

With the golden glow of the candlelight kissing his cheeks, he hovered over a spirit mirror, a flat, exquisitely lustrous "shew-stone" fashioned out of raven-black obsidian. Gazing intently upon his reflection in the dark volcanic glass, he chanted in hushed tones as he ran his fingers across the engravings on the oat-colored wax wheel next to him, the Sigilla iEmeth, which featured a septogram and runic carvings and symbols in minuscule print. Contrary to what one might expect, it was not a phantom, hobgoblin, or demon that he sought, but rather, the seraphic voice, and perhaps even the face of an angel – the one bridge between mankind and their Creator, one who holds the key to all of life's unanswerable questions.

Was this man delusional? Perhaps so, but perhaps not. But there was no question among those on hand that this was not an ignorant, philistine, unlettered buffoon of a man who readily boarded the train of groundless superstition. Far from it, this was a man who held not only a master's degree, but a doctorate, and his simultaneously stimulating and mesmerizing lectures drew crowds of royals and nobles from near and far. This was a man who was well-versed in a host of academic fields, and he would go on to serve as one of his queen's foremost personal advisers. He was also a prolific author whose revolutionary ideas helped charted the path for the burgeoning British Empire.

The man in question is none other than John Dee, one of the greatest scientific minds of his time, but also one of the most controversial. He was a learned man in fields as varied as mathematics and astronomy, centuries before they became formalized fields of study, but he is better remembered for performing magic and alchemy. Instead of astronomy, he became renowned across England for astrology, and he was one of the country's most notorious occult writers during his life.

Given the variety that the Elizabethan Era had to offer, it should come as little surprise that some eccentric characters with seemingly unique skills pushed to the forefront and became lauded members of society. Over the course of her long reign, Queen Elizabeth I became one of England's most famous and influential rulers, and it was an age when the arts, commerce, and trade flourished. It was the epoch of gallantry and great, enduring literature. It was also an age of wars and military conflicts in which men were the primary drivers and women often were pawns.

Queen Elizabeth I changed the rules of the game and indeed she herself was changed by the game. She was a female monarch of England, a kingdom that had unceremoniously broken with the Catholic Church, and the Vatican and the rest of Christendom was baying for her blood. She had had commercial and militaristic enemies galore. In the end, she helped change the entire structure of female leadership.

Elizabeth was the last Tudor sovereign, the daughter of the cruel and magnificent King Henry VIII and a granddaughter of the Tudor House's founder, the shrewd Henry VII. Elizabeth, hailed as "Good Queen Bess," "Gloriana" and "The Virgin Queen" to this day in the public firmament, would improve upon Henry VIII's successes and mitigate his failures, and despite her own failings would turn out to "have the heart and stomach of a king, and a king of England too". Indeed, that was the phrase she would utter in describing herself while exhorting her troops to fight for England against the Spanish Armada.

Elizabeth often has been featured in biographies that were more like hagiographies, glossing over her fits of temper, impatience and other frailties. It is fair to say, however, that she had also inherited her grandfather's political acumen and her father's magnificence, thus creating not just one of the most colorful courts in Europe but also one of the most effective governments in English history. It was an age of Christopher Marlowe's and William Shakespeare's flourishing creativity that still enhances English as well as comparative literature. Elizabeth was also the patroness of Sir Francis Drake, the pirate, thereby promoting English settlement of foreign colonies. The Jamestown settlement in Virginia would come in 1607, four years after Elizabeth's death, and the Plymouth colony in Massachusetts would come in 1620.

Those fledgling attempts at settlements were among the first to herald the dawn of the British Empire, and John Dee himself has been credited with coming up with the name "British Empire" in the first place. As all of this suggests, to say that John Dee was a storied man would be a grave understatement, to say the least. His multifaceted reputation preceded him, and his name became synonymous with both brilliance and disconcerting eccentricity. By all means, he certainly looked the part - the occultist towered over his peers, his wiry frame cloaked in a charcoal-black "artist's gown" with a ruffled white collar, his veined hands peeking out of his flared sleeves. He bore a pasty, pallid complexion, which seemed almost ghostly, paired with a magnificent beard that was "as white as milk."

Chilling rumors about his immeasurable magical abilities have kept his name alive for centuries. Legend has it that this was a man who singlehandedly cast a crippling curse on the Spanish Armada as the fleet sailed towards England, conjuring up the merciless storms and violent waves that threatened to swallow the ill-starred convoy whole, and left them with no choice but to turn back. This was a man who was once branded "the greatest rogue in the neighborhood of London," and who allegedly inspired the characters of Doctor Faustus from Christopher Marlowe's Elizabethan tragedy, as well as Prospero in William Shakespeare's *The Tempest*.

Indeed, Dee was, as they say, a mystery wrapped in an enigma, but how did he come to acquire such an impressive and frightful reputation? And how did this unusual individual rise to become one of the queen's most important advisors? *John Dee: The Life and Legacy of the English Occultist, Alchemist, and Philosopher Who Became Queen Elizabeth I's Spiritual Advisor* chronicles the unique work Dee did in various fields during the 16th century, and the lasting legacy he left on the British Empire. Along with pictures of important people, places, and events, you will learn about John Dee like never before.

John Dee: The Life and Legacy of the English Occultist, Alchemist, and Philosopher Who Became Queen Elizabeth I's Spiritual Advisor

About Charles River Editors

Introduction

    The Seeds of Unfathomable Wisdom

    The Queens

    The Trouble With Scryers

    Dee's Final Years

    Online Resources

    Further Reading

Free Books by Charles River Editors

Discounted Books by Charles River Editors

The Seeds of Unfathomable Wisdom

"What I say is not of myself: neither that which is said to me is of themselves: but it is said of him who liveth forever." – John Dee, On the Mystical Rule of Seven Planets (1583)

It was the 13th of July in the year 1527 when a young Welsh couple in Tower Ward, London welcomed what would be their only child. The couple cooed and fussed over the boy, named Jonathan, as they swaddled the precious infant, completely oblivious to the power and influence the rosy-cheeked, twinkling-eyed baby would one day possess, as well as the darkness and apparent devilry that would forever shroud his name. That said, there were a few who would, in hindsight, beg to differ. The child was born on the 13th, a number many in the West superstitiously consider unlucky, particularly amongst Christians, due to Judas Iscariot, the guest who shattered the even 12 in attendance at the Last Supper. What's more, the surname Dee was a derivative of the Welsh term *du*, meaning "black."

Dee's father, Rowland Dee, who originally hailed from Radnorshire in east-central Wales, juggled quite a few titles. He was primarily a royal textile merchant, importer, and sewer, meaning he not only traded fabrics, but was tasked with purchasing, supplying, and at times even producing some of the threads worn by the monarch and other members of the royal family. He served as a minor courtier to King Henry VIII, and he was later granted the post of "King's Packer." When he was older, John later claimed that his father Rowland was a descendant (through his paternal grandfather, Bedo Dee) of Rhodri Mawr, also known as Roderick the Great, the 9th century king of Gwynedd. In some accounts, Dee also claimed to share a lineage with King Arthur Pendragon, who presided over the knightly fellowship of the Round Table.

Very little is known about the Dee matriarch, Jane (in some accounts, Johanna) Wild. She was the daughter of a man named William Wild, presumably a relatively wealthy man who later chipped in with Dee's tuition fees. She married Rowland at the age of 15, and she gave birth to John three years later, after which she most likely assumed the duties of a traditional housewife. Dee would later make a brief and rare reference to his mother on the back of a 1547 horoscope guide penned by Girolamo Cardano. The snippet reads: "Anno 1508 vel 1509 on Crispinians day 21 [sic] Octobris, my mother was borne, to whome I am very like in visnomy (physiognomy), saving my nares (nose)."

One can safely assume that Dee's childhood was a semi-privileged one. He may not have been gorging himself on lavish spreads for all three meals, nor did he have a retinue of maids and butlers who waited on him hand and foot, but he also never felt the paralyzing pangs of hunger, and he was blessed with the means to pursue multiple levels of education. Indeed, the boy was not one to squander such an opportunity, and even as a young lad, Dee showed plenty of promise, and then some. He was bright, naturally inquisitive, and clearly gifted, learning the complex rules of grammar and the Latin language when he was no older than four or five.

This was just scratching the surface of his profound intellect. Shortly after his ninth birthday, Dee's parents decided it was time to tap into his potential, so they enrolled him at the Chelmsford Chantry School in Essex, thus beginning the first phase of his formal education. It was here that Dee became acquainted with reading, writing, arithmetic, and other fundamentals, and where he further enriched his understanding of Latin.

In November 1542, the then 15-year-old Dee left the grammar school in Essex and proceeded to St. John's College, a constituent college of the University of Cambridge. It was here, as Dee himself explained in his autobiography, that he truly began to appreciate his education and became an unflaggingly conscientious student. In addition to furthering his already masterful knowledge of Latin, the teenager applied himself to the subjects of grammar, rhetoric, and logic, as well as Greek, Hebrew, geometry, astronomy, music, and the three philosophies (Natural, Moral, and Divine). The latter unquestionably strengthened his religiosity.

The academic atmosphere was intensely competitive, and the institution proved to be a breeding ground for scholars, statesmen, and all-around influential individuals. Dee studied alongside William Cecil, the future two-term Secretary of State and Lord High Treasurer who also became a chief adviser for Queen Elizabeth I. Another pupil was William Grindal, later employed as a private tutor for Princess Elizabeth. He was responsible for her proficiency in Greek and Latin. Then there was James Pilkington, author, orator, the first Protestant bishop of Durham, and future founder of Rivington Grammar School. Dee was also under the private tutelage of Sir John Cheke, the first crown-appointed Greek professor at the University of Cambridge.

Cecil

An engraving of Grindal

An engraving of Cheke

Dee detailed the rigid routine he kept to maintain his place at the front of the pack throughout his time at St. John's: "In the years 1543, 1544, [and] 1545, I was so vehemently bent to study, that for those years I did inviolably keep this order: only to sleep four hours every night; to allow to meat and drink (and some refreshing after) two hours every day; and of the other 18 hours all (except the time of going to and being at divine service) was spent in my studies and learning."

When Dee was due to graduate from St. John's, his father's career took a sharp downturn, which culminated in his political and financial ruin. The senior Dee was understandably skeptical about allowing his son to pursue more education, but John's grandfather, William, recognized the greatness his grandson was bound to achieve and encouraged him to resume his studies by paying his tuition. Thus, Dee received his bachelor's degree from St. John's in the spring of 1546.

In the winter months of the same year, King Henry VIII inaugurated the newly-founded Trinity College, and the 19-year-old was among the first batch of students to receive a coveted invitation to become a fellow of the soon-to-be prestigious establishment and commence work on his master's degree. Dee, at this stage well-versed in Greek, was also designated as a Greek under-reader, a sort of understudy to the primary reader, Robert Pember.

King Henry VIII

Dee had always attracted the admiration and occasional envy of his professors and peers alike, but it was during his stint as a stage manager and carpenter for the students' rendition of *Elprjvri*, a renowned comedy by the 5th century CE playwright Aristophanes, that he first showcased the true depths of his ingenuity. To some, it was even a foreshadowing of his incalculable magical prowess.

For the production, Dee engineered what most modern chroniclers now believe to be a manpowered crane or some other similar contraption that would allow the character Trygseus to "take flight." Trygseus, who saw fit to confer with Zeus about the prospective military campaigns of the Athenians, was seen mounting a mechanical beetle named Scarabaeus (of Dee's creation), carrying with him a basket brimming with food and ascending to the god's palace of clouds hovering over the stage. By today's standards, this would have been considered a strong, but simple special effect, typically with the utilization of a counterweight fly system. In the 16th century, however, audiences were completely unaccustomed to the illusion, and many in the audience were so overwhelmed by the dazzling effect that they were convinced it involved the paranormal. Despite the sensation he generated, Dee later brushed off the innovative effect as nothing more than a "boyish attempt."

In addition to this breathtaking stage illusion, Dee also experimented with the contrivance of a perpetual motion machine with Gerolamo Cardano, an Italian polymath and founder of the concept of probability. Together, they carried out trials on an unidentified gem that was purported to possess otherworldly properties, but due to creative differences, the pair eventually jettisoned their ambitious projects.

An engraving of Cardano

It was also during his time at Trinity that Dee dove into what is now generally regarded as alternative sciences. He became besotted with astronomy and celestial navigation, and he recalled recording "thousands of observations (...to the hour and minute) of heavenly influences and operations actual in this elemental portion of the world." All his observations were carefully charted and later published in special tables called "ephemerides." Though he was a devout Christian, his astronomical studies kindled an obsession within him, an intense longing for answers that could only be found beyond the material world. Dee also devoted plenty of time and effort to studying the fields of general navigation, cartography, and medicine, and he became even more interested in the fascinating science behind mathematics.

In May 1547, Dee ventured abroad for the first time to link up with academics from various Dutch universities to deliberate over mathematics. Most of his time was spent in the Low Countries, where he encountered and forged friendships with a number of experts in the field, including the celebrated mapmaker and founder of the Netherlandish school of cartography, Gemma Frisius. He also met Antonius Gogava, a physician and translator of Greek treatises, and the legendary Gerard Mercator, the cartographer, geographer, and cosmographer who created the cylindrical Mercator projection. After meeting these men and other esteemed philosophers and intellectuals, Dee returned to Cambridge bearing gifts for the fellows and students at Trinity: two spectacular globes modeled by Mercator himself, as well as a brass staff and an armillary ring, also known as a "Gemma ring," an astronomical instrument used by Frisius himself (hence its nickname).

A picture of one of Mercator's globes (1551)

Frisius

Upon his return to Cambridge in early 1548, Dee wrapped up his master's studies, which he secured on April 14 along with a glowing testimonial from the Vice Chancellor and Convocation that attested to his superior grades and exemplary conduct. He cherished the certificate and brought it along with him on his second tour abroad. Three months later, Dee arrived in Louvain, Belgium, just 16 miles east of Brussels, and enrolled himself as a student at the University of Louvain just in time for the start of the midsummer term. He studied there for the next two years, with a focus on mathematics, geography, and cartography.

While he was studying those physical sciences, Dee became acquainted with and then engrossed in the art of alchemy. It was apparently the gripping manuscripts of the well-traveled German scholar, theologian, and once-secretary to Emperor Maximilian, Henricus Cornelius Agrippa, that pushed him into the arcane world of alchemy and the occult. In the *De occulta philosophia* series, the three-volume series claimed that God had, as broken down by author R. Schmitz, "created several worlds [from the void], three of which constitute the All: the domain of the elements, the heavenly world of the stars, and the intelligible cosmos of the angels." Dee was so smitten with Agrippa's ideas that he was said to have virtually memorized the entire breadth of Agrippa's series, often quoting lengthy passages from his books. Dee's later work, *Mysteriorum Libri*, also made several references to the esoteric themes discussed in Agrippa's literature.

An engraving of Agrippa

Naturally, Dee's illustrious professors, including Frisius, were most impressed by his boundless intellect and his extraordinary capacity for thinking outside the box. He acquired his doctoral diploma in the spring of 1550, and he was thereby addressed as "Dr. Dee" for the first time.

Shortly after he received his doctoral degree, Dee found himself behind a podium for the first time, conducting his first lecture in mathematics. He was clearly a natural, and his audience took to him almost immediately, drawn not only to his deep knowledge and passion for the subject, but also to his effortless confidence and charisma. Along with his commanding diction, Dee later coined and introduced the mathematical symbols +, -, ÷, and x to England.

Having stumbled into his niche, the aspiring lecturer journeyed to Paris on July 20, 1550, and proceeded to carry out a number of free public lectures centered on Euclid's *Elements* at the College of Rheims. His disquisitions were smash hits that drew tremendous audiences, many of them well-established names in the field with far more experience, and as word about his stimulating lectures spread, more people began to queue up outside of the lecture hall hours before the presentation. Eventually, so many people showed up that the auditorium could no longer contain them, and eager attendees who failed to squeeze into the hall resorted to clawing their way up to the windows, where they could be granted a glimpse of the highly sought-after speaker.

Dee continued on with his tour across Europe and conducted more spellbinding lectures, chiefly on mathematics and philosophy, before even larger audiences. He began to spot the faces of nobles and even royals in the awestruck crowd. Charlotte Fell Smith, author of the aptly-named *John Dee, 1527-1608* biography, listed a few of these important attendees: "Italian and Spanish nobles; the dukes of Mantua and Medina Celi; the Danish king's mathematician, Mathias Hacus; and his physician, Joannes Capito; Bohemian students...[and] a distinguished Englishman, Sir William Pickering, afterwards ambassador to France."

Dee's seemingly incontrovertible expertise earned him countless job offers, including the patronage of multiple European monarchs. King Henri II of France extended to him the post of King's Mathematical Reader, with a stipend of 200 crowns per annum. Other competitive offers came from Holy Roman Emperor Charles V, Tsar Ivan the Terrible, and Monseigneurs Babeu, de Rohan and de Monluc, among others. Still, Dee, who envisioned a career in his motherland, politely dismissed these opportunities. His household name status in Paris also granted him access to the inner circles of more European scholars such as French astronomer and physician Antoine Mizauld; mathematician and cartographer Oronce Finé, Italian humanist and mathematician Federico Commandino, and Flemish Roman Catholic theologian Francis Sylvius.

Upon Dee's return to England in December 1551, his former professor Sir Cheke introduced him to William Cecil. By then, Dee had already completed two more manuscripts, *De usi Globi Celestis* and *De nubium, solis, lunce, ac religorum planetarum*, which Cheke had used as lesson books during his tutelage of the king. These books, which were dedicated to the monarch, not only placed him in the good graces of the king, but also earned him a small annual stipend of 100 crowns. That stipend aside, the king also purchased a number of books for Dee's growing collection, an arrangement that lasted until his demise.

In 1552, Dee accepted the patronages of the Earl of Pembroke and John Dudley, the 1st Duke of Northumberland. He was employed as a private tutor to the children of the latter, who specifically sought "the best scientific education in England." Dee also moonlighted as a private instructor in the fields of mathematics, navigation, and astronomy, and later served as an on-call advisor for the Muscovy Company, the first major chartered joint stock company in the country. His roster of students for the next three decades included: explorer and Parliament member Humphrey Gilbert; poet, politician, and courtier William Raleigh; explorer and navigator Richard Chancellor; privateer Martin Frobisher; scholar and soldier Philip Sidney; comptroller of the Royal Navy William Borough; and William's brother, arctic explorer Stephen Borough. In return for his stellar services, Dee was granted the rectory of Upton upon Severn, a quaint town in what is now the Malvern Hills District of Worcestershire.

On July 6, 1553, the wretched malady of tuberculosis claimed Dee's most prominent patron, King Edward VI. Lady Jane Grey, who was appointed Edward's heir prior to his death, rose to the throne on July 10, but Grey was an unwilling participant in this convoluted scheme. She had apparently been hoodwinked into the position by being urged to try on the crown "to see how it would fit." Upon donning the bejeweled tiara, she was declared Queen of England.

The turmoil, however, had only just begun. Following much persuasion from Mary Tudor's supporters, including the Earl of Pembroke, who unsheathed his sword in a bid to prevail upon the members of the Privy Council, Grey was deposed on July 19. Her self-proclaimed replacement, Mary I, gladdened the unsuspecting public, who deemed the Tudor, previously rendered illegitimate due to the annulment of Henry VIII and Catherine of Aragon's marriage, the rightful heir to Edward's throne. Not long after Mary's acquisition of the crown, Dudley was convicted of high treason and promptly executed, a somber presage of Mary's turbulent reign.

Bloody Mary

Notwithstanding Dee's close ties to the duke, he was not persecuted, cushioned by his then-impeccable reputation and affiliations with a number of notable names in Parliament. As it turned out, however, this immunity would be short-lived, and it would not be long before the public turned on Dee himself, transforming the once beloved polymath into an evil enchanter and enemy of the state.

The Queens

"Perspective is an art mathematical which demonstrates the manner and properties of all radiations direct, broken, and reflected." – attributed to John Dee

The new queen's infamous and indelible nickname, "Bloody Mary," which would cling to her for centuries to come, was no accident. In her zeal to terminate the Protestant Reformation and have England forcibly revert back to Catholicism, an estimated 300 "religious dissenters" and "heretics" were burnt at the stake. As if the harrowing slaughter, now known as the "Marian persecutions," was not enough, the ashes of the corpses were then tossed into the river to prevent their loved ones from fashioning relics out of their remains.

Most were asphyxiated by the rippling clouds of smoke, but not all were so fortunate. Bishop Nicholas Ridley of London and Westminster, for instance, who was targeted for his teachings and unapologetic endorsement of Lady Grey, suffered miserably, squirming and screeching in abject agony as the flames engulfed his feet. He was heard crying, "Lord have mercy upon me, intermedling this cry, let the fire come unto me, I cannot burn..."

In February 1554, Sir Thomas Wyatt the Younger, the son and namesake of the revered lyric poet, spearheaded 4,000 men on a march across London, determined to oust Mary from her throne and replace her with her half-sister Elizabeth. Much to the dismay of these insurgents, the rebellion was crushed not long after it began, and Wyatt, along with roughly 90 of the rebels were executed. Elizabeth and Edward Courtenay, the 1st Earl of Devon and Elizabeth's alleged suitor, were implicated as Wyatt's fellow conspirators, and both were held in the Tower of London. Furthermore, Lady Grey, who was deemed a menace to Mary's authority, was charged with high treason, laid down on the scaffold, and decapitated. Many have argued that Mary's killing streak, while indisputably abhorrent, was minor in comparison to that of her father, who supposedly massacred some 70,000 souls throughout his 38-year reign, and that her sobriquet was therefore somewhat excessive. Nevertheless, it was clear that the temperamental and unsparing queen was not one to be trifled with lightly.

Not long after the unraveling of Wyatt's rebellion, Oxford fellows Richard Bruern and Richard Smith reached out to Dee and offered him the post of reader of Mathematical Sciences, but Dee rejected the post. Dee was then preoccupied with other literary projects, and he had just published a number of treatises the previous year, including *The Philosophical and Political Occasions and Names of the Heavenly Asterismes* and *The Cause of Floods and Ebbs*, as per the request of the Duchess of Northumberland. He was also in the midst of writing other dissertations. Dee was displeased with the university's prioritization of grammar and rhetoric over science and philosophy, and he felt that this dissonance would be much too large an obstacle to overcome.

The following year, Dee was admitted to the Mercers' Company of London, a post he inherited from his father, a former member of the institution. This provided him with access to the organization's merchants, and it also allowed him to forge a relationship with the well-established and influential Loks, who later sought out his nautical and geographical expertise for their enterprises. From his mother, Dee later inherited the Mortlake estate, which neighbored Richmond Palace. Not only did the Mortlake manor serve as his primary place of residence in his later years, it also served as a strong leverage for his mortgages and loans.

In the summer of 1555, Dee was summoned to draw up a birth chart for Queen Mary. Shortly thereafter, he began to exchange letters with Princess Elizabeth, then based in Woodstock, who also requested a reading of her horoscope. Dee obliged, and from the session he concluded that Elizabeth would soon rise to the throne and be blessed with a long, prosperous reign, whereas Mary would meet a bleak end.

Princess Elizabeth

Though Dee and Elizabeth intended to keep the contentious results to themselves, word of the astrologer's troubling calculations leaked. A man by the name of George Ferrys approached Queen Mary, claiming that Dee had cast a string of wicked spells directed at the monarch, and that the sorcerer had inflicted a demonic enchantment upon his sons, robbing one of his vision and the other of his life. Following this revelation, soldiers were dispatched to Dee's home in London, where, under the queen's instructions, they proceeded to seal up the residence and rummage through his belongings. Dee was consequently shackled and imprisoned at the Tower, charged with witchcraft and high treason, or more specifically, for "attempting to calculate the nativities, and predicting the death of royals."

Dee was tasked with defending himself before the Secretary of State and other members of the Privy Council at the Star Chamber. The astute astrologer succeeded in convincing the council of his innocence and was released three months later on August 29, 1555, whereupon he was scheduled to appear before Bishop Bonner for another line of questioning. Much to Dee's relief, he managed to appease the bishop's concerns regarding his religiosity. In fact, Dee was so charming that he managed to strike up a friendship with the bishop that lasted until his death.

However, Dee would never be able to escape the scandalous epithets of "necromancer" and "conjurer of evil spirits," which hounded him for the rest of his life. He often bemoaned the injustice of his disrepute, which seemed to stem from his passion for esoteric sciences. His despair was captured in a preface he penned for the English translation of Euclid's Elements, in which he complained, "I seek the treasure of heavenly wisdom and knowledge. So why do they condemn me as a companion of hell hounds and a caller and conjurer of wicked and damned spirits?"

Dee released his first printed publication – a preface to John Field's *Ephemeris anni 1557* – at the start of 1556, and on January 15 of that year, he embarked on what would be one of his most noteworthy projects. In an entreaty addressed to Queen Mary, suitably, yet wordily titled "A Supplication for the Recovery and Preservation of Ancient Writers and Monuments," he denounced the government's deliberate disbandment of the nation's monasteries, which resulted in the demolition of monastic libraries. In the process, its priceless literary collections were either reduced to ashes or forever lost under the rubble. He petitioned the queen to erect a proper national library that would house what was left of these prized collections, and to allow him to procure new books and duplicate surviving manuscripts.

He hoped to persuade the queen through a number of tactical arguments. First and foremost, by authorizing a national library, the queen could possibly salvage her reputation. In that way, her enduring contribution would literally be one for the history books. Moreover, a communal library would allow citizens from all walks of life access to a variety of literature that was then only reserved for nobles, privileged owners of private libraries, and those in the upper echelons of society.

Dee also outlined a plan that would make such an endeavor attainable. A commission would first be established, responsible for scouting out rare surviving manuscripts. A second team of scribes would then replicate said manuscripts by hand before returning the original books to their respective owners. Dee suggested that the salaries of the staff be jointly financed by Lord Chancellor and Archbishop of York, Nicholas Heath, and the clergymen and laymen of Canterbury Province. He also proposed that the synod oversee and perform the administrative duties of the project in the time leading up to the completion of the library.

Regrettably, Dee's proposal to preserve "the treasure of all antiquity and the everlasting seeds of continual excellency within...Your Grace's realm" was rebuffed. Disenchanted, but undeterred, Dee continued to purchase these precious manuscripts on his own dime, and he took it upon himself to recreate borrowed copies, which included Thomas Norton's *The Ordinal of Alchemy*, Roger Bacon's *On Burning Lenses*, and the *Ashmole Beastiary*, a 12th century illuminated manuscript that was essentially a creation story coupled with an assortment of "allegorical" portrayals of more than 100 animals. And thus began Dee's legendary library at the Mortlake manor. The crackerjack polymath, over time, amassed over 4,000 individual texts. His many friends and contacts often swung by for a cup of tea and a gander at his remarkable collection.

On November 17, 1558, Mary I succumbed to complications stemming from either uterine cancer or ovarian cysts. The melodious peals of church bells that filled the streets and the mirthful dancing that followed were just as jubilant, if not more so than the gaiety that transpired when she was initially crowned. This led to one of the most defining moments in Dee's eminent career. Apart from the publication of his *Propaedeumata aphoristica*, a short compendium consisting of 120 aphorisms regarding cosmology, astrology, and natural philosophy, he was presented with a monumental task.

Elizabeth, as Dee had seemingly predicted, was now next in line for the vacant throne. The polymath was summoned to the chamber of Robert Dudley, 1st Earl of Leicester, and it was requested that the astrologer consult the stars and draw up an "electional chart" so as to select a propitious date for Elizabeth's impending coronation in Westminster Abbey. Dee did as he was told, and after some deep rumination, he settled upon the 15th (in some accounts, 14th) of January, 1559. Sarah Rochel, author of *The Queen's Astrologer*, spelled out the significance of Dee's astrological calculations: "One of the working principles of astrology is that the beginnings of life – the birth of something or the seed of something – is of paramount importance. It signals the way things will develop and unfold in time. An astrological birth chart, therefore, can not only be used to examine the start of a person's life...but can also be applied to, say, the start of a journey; the laying of a foundation stone; [or] the signing of a contract."

In the following passage, Sue Toohey, who penned "Elizabeth I, the Virgin Queen," described the results of Elizabeth's electional chart: "Elizabeth's transits to her natal chart at the time of the coronation included Jupiter sextile Jupiter, which became exact on the day of her coronation along with Venus trine her Sun, making it a very pleasant occasion. Venus opposed Saturn and, Mars was conjunct her Mars ruled [Medium Coeli/Midheaven] showing that she would not be a weak and feeble monarch, but one who would rule with great fortitude...Uranus was on her MC and Mars was trine Uranus. This would bring dynamic leadership and great self-determination to her rule. She would not be constrained by what others had done before her, and would create her own style of rule."

Dee's highly palatable calculations, as well as his exceptional work ethic, ensured him a retainer as a royal consultant in various fields for the following two decades.

Despite what Dee had prophesied, Queen Elizabeth's otherwise fruitful reign was marred by her poor health – the monarch frequently fell ill and flirted with death on three separate occasions – and a lack of confidence that was often bolstered by a stalwart support system. On top of deciphering planetary positions, comets, eclipses, and other duties expected of a Royal

Astrologer, Dee was employed as the queen's "Noble Intelligencia." As one might imagine, he was also first to respond to all matters of the inexplicable and supernatural.

One fateful morning sometime thereafter, court and council members burst into a contagious ripple of panic when a royal attendant came upon a startling sight: a wax sculpture modeled in the queen's likeness, discovered with an ominous pin speared in its chest. The hexed figurine, they gathered, presaged the prolonged and painful, yet inevitable erosion and demise of Queen Elizabeth. Messengers from all directions frantically mounted their horses and raced to the Mortlake estate. Thankfully, Dee eventually determined it was a false alarm, describing the doll as a cruel but ultimately harmless practical joke.

Dee's relationship with Elizabeth only became more firmly rooted with time. One of Henry Gillard Glindoni's most acclaimed masterpieces, *John Dee Performing an Experiment Before Queen Elizabeth I*, perfectly encapsulates the unconventional but nonetheless profound friendship between the two. In this painting, Dee, depicted in an onyx-black robe, is seen pouring the contents of an unidentifiable vial into a crucible containing a blinding white flame. Elizabeth, depicted in full golden and bejeweled regalia, is seated upon her royal red-throne, surrounded by her gawking cortege and looking on in quiet amazement. In a symbolic twist, an x-ray scan in 2016 revealed an astonishing element that had been suspiciously eliminated from the original version of the painting: a ring of human skulls that encircled Dee's figure.

The painting

There was no doubt that confidentiality was an important ingredient in their unlikely bond. When Dee and Elizabeth wished to convey a message that they could not afford to be exposed, they communicated via secret code. Dee signed off as "007" – the "00" represented a set of eyes, presumably as in "for your eyes only," and "7" was Dee's lucky number. One would be correct to assume that Dee's code name directly inspired the alias of Ian Fleming's James Bond character.

There were plenty of whispers regarding the true nature of their relationship, with many of them insisting that the pair were intimately involved. There has been little to no evidence that substantiates this notion, and their relationship was most likely purely platonic.

Dee's triumphant and expeditious rise in the wake of Elizabeth's coronation could not satiate Dee's addictive disposition. He had toiled away in his study for years, buried up to his neck in dusty books and manuscripts, and endlessly scribbling until he could no longer feel the quill against his calloused and paper-cut-ridden fingers. Still, he had not found the answers he had been yearning for. Or perhaps he had simply been looking in the wrong places – or rather, wrong books – all this time.

In early 1562, Dee returned to Louvain. As soon as he had made his rounds touching base with old acquaintances, he set out to commission the printing of a stack of manuscripts he had tucked away in his luggage. He also hunted down book collectors in the far-flung corners of serpentine alleyways and the city fringes for rare gems that could not be found in England. He also may have begun to expand his collection of Hebrew texts at this time.

In spite of Dee's best efforts, he failed to complete the progress he had hoped to achieve and journeyed to Antwerp that year with a heavy heart, until he chanced upon a Hungarian nobleman who sold to him a copy of *Steganographia*. The puzzling manuscript, written by the 15th century German Benedictine abbot and occultist Johannes Trithemius, revolved around the art of hidden messages and ciphers, and it claimed to unveil the secrets behind both cryptography and Enochian magic. Dee's excitement is palpable in the following excerpt of his letter to Cecil: "A book for your honor or a Prince, so meet, so needful and commodious, as in human knowledge none can be meeter or more behovfull [sic]...This book...I give unto your Honor as the most precious jewel that I have yet of other men's travels recovered."

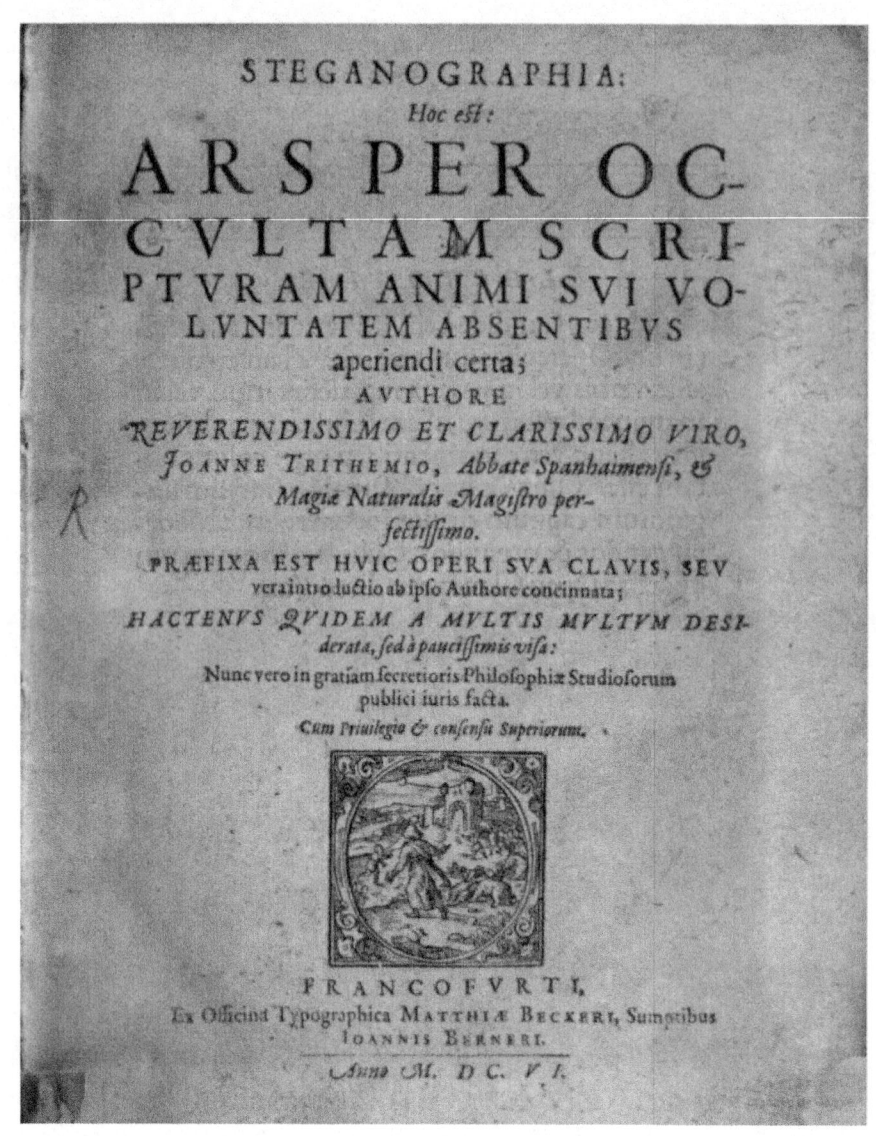

Title page from an early 17th century version of *Steganographia*

Dee glowed at the thought of his phenomenal find. Decrypting these ciphers, he believed, would vest in him the power to better visualize the future, which could be used to the advantage of British rulers and voyagers alike. At the same time, he was convinced that he could secure the alchemical formulas for transforming metals into gold, as well as immortality. He spent the following 10 days in his room, vigorously copying the lengthy manuscript by hand, and even then he completed only half of the book at most. When another wealthy aristocrat learned of Dee's predicament, he presented to Dee the following proposal: he would complete the remaining half of *Steganographia* should the polymath agree to remain in Antwerp and provide him with private instruction for a set time. Dee accepted this proposal.

Dee fulfilled his contract in the spring of 1563, whereupon he headed over to Zurich. It was here that he first met Swiss naturalist Conrad Gesner, who acquainted him with the work of an early 16th-century alchemist named Paracelsus. Dee would later become one of the men who transported Paracelsus's ideas – which included theories concerning the fabled Philosopher's Stone, as well as the Greek concept of the four elements and their connection to alchemy – throughout the continent. From Zurich, Dee scaled the Alps and entered Italy, traveling to Padua, Chiavenna, Venice, and Urbino before crossing over to Pressburg in Bratislava to see the coronation of the Hungary's King Maximilian I.

Dee returned to Antwerp in 1564, and while there he released *Monas Hieroglyphica* (*Hieroglyphic Monad*), a commentary on the esoteric symbol that he had designed, on the 24th of January. The hieroglyph – a Venus symbol with a dot enclosed within, perhaps representative of an eye, crowned with a sliver of a crescent on its back – demonstrated the marriage of "alchemy, Pythagorean numerology, textual Qabalah, and pious mysticism," an underlying theme woven into the strands of the cosmos and all of creation. One can only imagine Dee's disappointment when critics panned his opus by the droves. He later lamented, "University graduates of high degree, and other gentlemen dispraised it because they understood it not." He was able to find some solace in the fact "Her Majesty graciously defended credit in my absence beyond the seas."

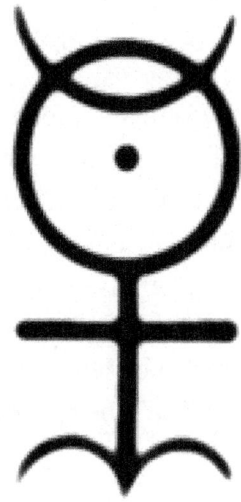

The glyph

That upcoming winter, Dee returned to Oxfordshire and resettled into his Mortlake home, where he resumed on the expansion of his soon-to-be renowned library, which would one day be the second largest collection in all of Europe. In addition to the dizzying volumes he already possessed, he found more on every scientific field imaginable, ranging from classic Roman poetry and Hermetic philosophical literature to unique alchemical texts from the medieval period. These priceless books aside, Dee also harbored an extensive collection of alchemical tools and a wide range of chemicals. Dee and his assistants conducted their experiments (and later, his scrying sessions) in a small network of sheds attached to the manor.

In 1565, Dee married a woman named Katherine Constable, and though their union lasted until her untimely death in 1574, their marriage produced no offspring. Little to nothing is known about the obscure Constable other than the fact that she had been previously married to an unnamed grocer. Dee was evidently not one to kiss and tell, seemingly choosing to refrain from revealing anything more than vague details regarding his romantic life in his journals.

During this time, Dee entertained scholarly and aristocratic visitors from near and far in his fashionable private library. At one point, Queen Elizabeth herself personally paid a visit to his Mortlake home, incidentally on the day of Constable's death. She opted to remain outside the premises upon being apprised of the tragic news.

In 1570, Dee completed an English translation of Euclid's *Elements of Geometrie*, along with a "Mathematical Preface" for it. His distinctive approach to the subject engendered much buzz within the field, especially the Mathesis concepts entwined in his ideas. Mathesis, in essence, was a Pythagorean-based, "mystical mathematics" that suggested the "mind of God" was composed of numbers, and thus that was how people could discover all the answers to the universe's questions. Only by employing magic to identify and solve the equations that would decode the "mind of God" can one unlock these answers. Dee also traveled to Lorraine and Paris to purchase more rare manuscripts and alchemical instruments during this time.

Although's Dee's second marriage (1575) to an unidentified woman also ended abruptly when she passed on from unknown causes in 1576, the year yielded him one small victory. Since 1563, the historian John Foxe, who played a crucial role in shaping society's perception of Bloody Mary, had been regularly releasing volumes, accompanied by highly detailed woodcuts of the series *Actes and Monuments*. The series, otherwise known as *Foxe's Book of Martyrs*, derogatorily referred to Dee as the "Great Conjurer" and was peppered with what he deemed to be slanderous and deleterious attacks on his character, mainly concerning his alleged practicing of dark magic. By 1571, Foxe's bestseller could be found on display in just about every church and cathedral, regardless of size, in England.

Crushed and incensed by the bad press, Dee wrote a public letter addressed to Foxe and his disparagers. "O, my unkind countrymen," read Dee's scathing letter. "O natural Countrymen, O [ungrateful] countrymen, o brain-sick, rash, spiteful, and disdainful countrymen. Why oppress you me thus violently with your slandering of me, contrary to verity, and contrary to your own conscience?...Have I so long, so dearly, so far, so carefully, so painfully, so dangerously fought and traveled for the learning of wisdom and attaining of virtue, and in the end am I become worse than when I began? Worse than a madman, a dangerous member in the Commonwealth and no Member of the Church of Christ?"

Dee's strongly-worded, but heartfelt pleas were finally heard, and all unflattering references to Dee were extracted from the 1576 installment of *Actes and Monuments*.

In 1577, Dee published *General and Rare Memorials Pertaining to the Perfect Art of Navigation*, a disruptive treatise that urged England to assert territorial claims in the New World. This would mean challenging Portugal and Spain, and Dee's work mapped out potential methods and benefits of achieving such a feat. Dee was keen for an opportunity to flex his lesser-known, but equally masterly fortes. On top of being a seasoned, royally certified stargazer and one of the continent's leading book collectors, Dee helped propel England into the Age of Exploration.

Dee proposed that the government retire or slow down their exploratory voyages into uncharted areas and instead concentrate on claiming (or reclaiming) territories that historically and rightfully belonged to Britain. He named certain North Atlantic islands, among them Frieseland (a province in the northern part of the Netherlands), that qualified, as well as the territories supposedly appropriated by King Arthur. Dee cited an old folklore centered on Madoc, which claimed that the Welsh prince sailed to America in 1170, three centuries prior to Columbus' voyage, thereby making the British rulers the true "owners" of the American coast and its nearby islands. By reacquiring and rebranding these territories into "The British Empire" – a term of Dee's creation – Britain's global power, he reasoned, would grow tenfold.

Between the 1550s and the 1570s, Dee's expertise in both astronomy and cartography landed him dozens of jobs as an adviser for British voyages. Those who were unschooled in sailing were taught by Dee both basic and complex techniques of celestial navigation. Dee's clients visited the Mortlake manor to refer to his maps and books on navigation, and the owner of the estate also actively provided tips and aided them with the plotting of their journeys.

Dee was especially committed to locating the Northwest Passage that Europeans believed would be the shortest route to Asia, and he even personally invested in a few of these voyages. Much to his agitation, none of these ventures ever took, and he never saw much, if anything of a return on these investments. Still, Dee quite enjoyed his consultation gigs, for he was able to exchange ideas with new faces and old friends, such as those of Philip Sidney and Humphrey Gilbert. When Dee served as adviser to one of Gilbert's voyages in the early 1580s, the adventurer compensated him with a deed to "all lands from the 50th parallel to the North Pole." If Gilbert had survived his return trip from this pivotal voyage, Dee would have been gifted with the deed to almost all of what is now Canada.

Gilbert

On February 5, 1578, 51-year-old Dee married Jane Fromond of East Cheam, Surrey, who was 28 years his junior. His 23-year-old bride made her bread and butter as a lady-in-waiting at the court of Lady Catherine Howard of Effingham. Lady Howard was the wife of Lord Admiral Charles Howard, who later commanded the royal fleet that defeated the previously indomitable Spanish Armada. In other accounts, Fromond was said to have served Elizabeth Fitzgerald, Countess of Lincoln, who herself was once a lady-in-waiting to Queen Elizabeth. Either way, Fromond resigned from her post shortly after their marriage was made official.

In defiance of the glaring age difference between them, as well as their conflicting personalities – Fromond was as intelligent and well-spoken as she was impulsive and fractious – the pair remained devoted to one another in sickness and in health. They went on to have eight children (according to some sources, 10).

It was at this stage that Dee began to keep a more comprehensive log of his daily life, and his documentation was so detailed that it contained mundane gems, such as a record of his children's hijinks: "1582, 3 July, Arthur fell from the top of the Watergate stayres [sic] and cut his forhead...1590, 5 August: Rowland fell into the Tems over head and eares about noone...1591, 27

June: Arthur wounded on his hed by his wanton throwing of a brik-bat upright and not well avoiding the fall of it again."

The pleasant monotony of his home life was, in all likelihood, a much-needed respite from the chaotic unrest that would plague him from then on out.

The Trouble With Scryers

"The learned will (no doubt) delight therein,

And their delight will draw them onto skill:

Admit the simple force it not a pin,

So much more the wise embrace it will." – John Dee

To Dee's contemporaries, there was a very fine line that lay between white and black magic. On the one hand, white magic was a pure and natural force of good, and it was a far more subtle entity, one defined by unexplainable workings brought about by unseen spiritual energies. Conversely, black magic was quite simply a force of evil that was either consciously or inadvertently summoned by enchanters for superstitious purposes or their own selfish gains. Dee was aware of the dangers that lurked in the act of walking this gossamer dividing line, but he was desperate. This risk was well-worth it, for he was seeking to achieve a full "understanding of the supracelestial virtues and metaphysical influences" that ruled the world of the unknown.

Dee's obsessive fascination with crystalomancy, or crystalgazing, which not only served as a mirror into the future, but also as a medium to converse with spirits and angels, heightened in the early 1580s. Irrespective of his fixation on the paranormal, he was, first and foremost, a cerebral, rational individual who knew the extent of his abilities. He had not been born with, nor did he ever acquire his third eye, often admitting unabashedly, "You know I cannot see, nor scry." If he wished to break through this mighty invisible wall, he would have to enlist the aid of a professional scryer.

Unfortunately, the scrying profession was littered with unscrupulous charlatans, and Dee, who possessed more academic smarts than he did street smarts, was easy prey. In the autumn of 1581, a phantom set of fingers began to pester the polymath by rapping its knuckles against the doors, cupboards, and windows in the dead of the night. The spooky occurrences coincided with uncannily vivid and disturbingly graphic nightmares. Understandably perturbed, yet also intrigued by these events, Dee employed Barnabas Saul to interpret what he believed to be a sign from God. Saul, a lay-preacher-turned-occultist with a shadowy past, listened patiently to Dee's woes and quickly agreed that these signs were indeed an omen sent down from the heavens. During the first consultation, the scryer's wandering eye landed on a crystal globe (in other sources, a piece of convex crystal) in Dee's study. The globe, shimmering under the golden rays of the sun, Dee explained, had been gifted to him by a friend. How very curious, the scryer remarked with a pensive look on his face, for this was the very instrument they required to communicate with the angels.

Saul and Dee's first scrying session, which the latter referred to as "Accio Saulina," took place on December 21, 1581. Upon gazing into the "great crystalline globe," Saul unveiled to Dee the rough coordinates of buried treasure: a chest containing rare manuscripts somewhere by Oundle in Northamptonshire. Dee hurried off to Oundle at once and searched high and low for this elusive chest, but he could find nothing of the like.

When the ornery Dee returned to Mortlake to confront Saul, the scryer, who was lodging at the chamber over the dining hall, exclaimed that he had been visited by "a spiritual creature" the previous evening. The apparition was not just of any winged creature, but Annael – one of the seven angels of creation. Annael relayed to Saul a special set of instructions to be carried out by the holder of the "sacred stone." On any day apart from the Sabbath, after "New Year's Tide," Dee, accompanied by Saul, was to take the globe and a shew-stone out on the brightest hour of the day and lay it under the sun. The pair were then to sit and kneel with the instruments and await further instructions. They waited and waited, but those instructions never came.

Dee eventually became bedeviled by suspicion, and, as it turned out, he had every right to be. On March 6, 1582, Saul made an attempt to dissolve the rocky partnership when he admitted that "he neither heard nor saw any spiritual creature anymore." The scryer was soon exposed as a fraud, at the insistence of Dee's friends, and he was accused of being a "plant" hired by Dee's enemies who hoped to frame the polymath for committing "indiscretions." A month or two later, Saul was arrested and tried in Westminster Hall, but to Dee's chagrin, Saul was acquitted. Dee later noted in his diary, "The injuries which this Barnabas had done me, diverse ways were very great."

Even so, the humiliation was not enough to boost his cynicism about scryers. On March 8, just two days after Saul's admission, Dee became acquainted with another spurious character by the name of Edward Talbot, one who was as deceptive as he was silver-tongued. Again, Dee became convinced that this chance encounter with yet another occultist had been orchestrated by the divine, because just the previous evening, Dee had attended a glorious exhibition of the mesmerizing Northern Lights.

Dee's wishful obliviousness to the 27-year-old scryer's true intentions was driven by his incorrigible desire to achieve what no other man has ever accomplished. For starters, the scryer, who only much later revealed his real surname to be "Kelley," hawked magical potions and alchemical elixirs for a living. He had no shortage of intellect, as he was once enrolled as an undergraduate at Oxford University, but he was disgracefully expelled for undisclosed reasons. Furthermore, he was more than conversational in Latin, adequate enough to charm Dee and his inner circle. But one glance at Kelley hinted at his duplicitous nature - his cropped ears, which were lopped off as punishment for his crime of coin-counterfeiting, were concealed under a black skullcap.

An engraving of Edward Kelley

In addition to Kelley's dubious track record were countless rumors regarding his skillful swindles. According to one such rumor, Kelley ushered a man and a few of his butlers into the Walton le Dale Park in Lancashire and terrorized them with well-scripted incantations. To further sell the illusion, Kelley led the impressionable victims to a freshly exhumed corpse, and, not unlike a depraved ventriloquist act, he imparted to the cowering men relatable proverbs pertaining to their futures.

One could attribute the aforementioned issues to Dee's ignorance of Kelley's shady past, but he also overlooked Kelley's unbecoming and telling behavior upon their first meeting. A glimpse of Kelley's manipulative disposition emerged when, within the first few minutes of their conversation, he began to badmouth Saul. Pay no attention to Saul's apprehension towards him, said Kelley. A "spiritual creature" had visited Kelley and instructed him to guide Dee in his endeavors, but also warned him of the derision Dee's chosen scryer (Saul) would spew about him. Kelley's unsavory opinion of Saul most likely played a significant role in Dee's decision to part ways with his first scryer.

March 10th, the date of Dee and Kelley's first scrying session, marked the beginning of what would be a seven-year partnership. The pair sat before a crystal globe, shew-stone in hand, and achieved a dramatically stunning breakthrough. Although Dee had expected a visit from Annael, it was instead an angel named Uriel, the "Spirit of Light," who appeared within the crystal. Uriel bore with him this message: Dee and Kelley were the chosen ones, handpicked to learn and disseminate the "language of the angels," which could only be accessed through a well-curated catalog of prayers and rituals. The pair could only accept this challenge if they vowed to "abuse not this excellency nor overshadow it with vanity, but stick firmly, absolutely and perfectly in the love of God for His honor, together."

In the years that followed, they sought out to unscramble the names of the "49 good angels, each beginning with the letter 'B'," as directed by Uriel, who would provide them with further clues and commands regarding the Enochian alphabet, as well as other secrets of the divine tongue. These angels are not to be confused with the messenger angels, such as Annael and Uriel, who delivered preliminary and closing messages and alerted them to threats and future occurrences of note. Dee must have been bursting at the seams with elation, believing that once he became fluent in Enochian, he would be granted a pass into the once-impenetrable realm of the angels.

On March 14th, Dee and Kelley were instructed by the messenger angel Michael to craft by hand an immaculate seal made from "clean, purified wax," measuring roughly 27 inches in circumference and 9 inches across. This was the inauguration of their first tangible project: the construction of a proper angel scrying station. Michael made certain to pop in daily in the days leading up to the 21st, reciting a list of the equipment needed for the scrying station in minute detail. That day, Kelley, supposedly enervated by all the séances, fell lightheaded, and was forced to terminate the session early.

The pair applied the finishing touches to the séance station on April 29th. Author Charlotte Fell Smith explained the final product: "[The] square table, 'the table of practice,' was...made of sweet wood and was about two cubits high, with four legs. On its sides [were] certain characters...to be written with sacred yellow oil, such as is used in churches. Each leg was...set upon a seal of wax made in the same pattern as the larger seal, the 'Sigilla iEmeth,' which was to be placed upon the center of the table."

The pair's calendars for the next two years were loaded with angelic séances and Enochian deciphering sessions. Contrary to what one might assume, there were no blood sacrifices, plumes of purifying smoke, bizarre dances, or demonic possessions. In reality, each session began with a solemn, silent prayer, asking meekly to be made worthy of the presence of God's beloved angels and the divine knowledge they were to about to receive.

Kelley's fingers danced along the Enochian symbols carved unto the Sigilla iEmeth as the patterns of a "magical square system" were revealed to him, powered by what Dee called the "De Heptarchia Mystica," or in English, "Heptarchic Magic." To receive the seven-lettered name of the 49 angels, the pair had to decrypt an intricate cross-shaped table consisting of 343 squares, split into smaller tables of seven, and further broken up into 49 squares. The pair also relied on the Sigilla iEmeth to spell out the instructions on the crafting of several magical and alchemical apparatuses; what's more, the Sigilla iEmeth provided them with succinct profiles of each of these angels, which included the specific powers and purposes of each angel.

This divine knowledge, said the messenger angels, was the same wisdom that God had once disclosed to Enoch, the seventh descendant of Adam, who in turn poured the wisdom into a book. When "wicked hands" sunk their claws into Enoch's book, however, the original copy was immediately destroyed. God was effectively traumatized and chose to never again impart this divine (and evidently dangerous) knowledge to mere mortals. That being said, Dee's prayers were apparently so impassioned and so profoundly earnest that God's faith in the matter was restored, once again deeming mankind to be worthy of this hallowed wisdom.

Dee kept his eyes glued to Kelley's flitting fingers and the carvings his fingertips kissed, studiously scrawling each symbol for over 100 separate séances. Over time, the angels also divulged recipes for immortality elixirs, among other magical mixtures, as well as instructions and clues to the location of the Philosopher's Stone. Dee was anxious to be vested with the supernatural powers the angels promised him, which they claimed would not only alter the political hierarchy of the entire continent, but would also enlighten them of the date of the upcoming Apocalypse (it was later deemed to be "in the year 88"). Dee therefore felt all the more obligated to keep meticulous records. Curiously, Dee never once referred to the angelic language as "Enochian," but instead preferred to use a variety of terms such as the Celestial Speech, the First Language of God-Christ, Adamical, or simply Angelical.

Rarely did Dee detect the physical presence of these angels, apart from the odd shaky table or flickering candles. Throughout all of these sessions, Dee never once saw or spoke to the angels himself, and he was no more than a secretary of sorts. Only Kelley, Dee's partner explained, had been gifted with the ability to see the angels "in sight," while Dee was destined to see them only "in faith." Still, Dee's optimism was unshakable.

More often than not, the angels appeared within the sacred stone. Occasionally, they floated out from a brilliant shaft of light that emanated from the stone and glided across the room. Sometimes, there was no apparition at all, only the sweet-toned, and sometimes booming voice of an angel drifted out of the stone. Both classes of angels often took on an androgynous form, but came in all shapes and sizes, from children and golden-locked, elderly women, to farmers cloaked in crimson and faceless, tall creatures.

A few angels even came complete with a full entourage. One who referred to himself as "King Carmara," donning a floor-length violet robe, appeared with a cortege of seven princes. Prince Bornogo materialized with a company of 42 magical ministers, and they astonished the scryer and his suggestible partner with a number of magic tricks before disintegrating into droplets of water and vanishing into thin air. An angel named Hagonel also arrived with 42 ministers. His frisky companions played a game of catch with hypnotically luminous "balls of gold," which were, in reality, "empty like a blown bladder." At times, the retinues that escorted these angels arranged themselves into meaningful letter formations, as depicted in the illustrations in Dee's journals.

The appearances of these obscure characters were punctuated with apparitions from a recurring cast of Biblical angels. There was the sword-wielding archangel Michael, guardian of Jacob and Israel, and appraiser of souls at Last Judgment, who appeared to the scryers on March 14, 1582. There was Raphael, who arrived the next day. He was the healer of earth and mankind, tasked with preserving the Tree of Life, and was among the seven angels of the Apocalypse. Then, there was Gabriel, most known for the visitation of Mary in Nazareth, who made his first appearance in late June of the following year. Gabriel was the guardian of Eden and the patron angel for resurrection, revelation, and annunciation. Dee felt a special kinship with Gabriel, for it was he who provided the recipe for the medicine that healed his ailing wife, Jane, later that year.

On May 13, 1583, a Polish nobleman named Adalbert Laski, Count Palatine of Siradz, traveled to the Mortlake estate. He presented Dee with small gifts from his travels in the hopes of picking the polymath's brain on occultist subjects, as well as being granted access to his one-of-a-kind library. Laski was overjoyed when Dee accepted his request, as he had trekked across all of England and visited its two most prominent universities in search of Dee, only to be disappointed by his absence. He explained, "I would not have come hither had I [known] that Dee was not here."

Shortly after Laski's arrival, he chose to push his luck and requested to be part of a séance, and to Laski's delight, an angel named Madini made a convenient appearance. Madini set herself apart from the rest of the apparitions in many ways. To start with, she took the form of a young girl, no more than nine years of age. She wore a frilly red dress of ruby-red and emerald-green, and skipped about the furniture and heaps of books Dee had yet to file away.

Despite her chipper demeanor, Madini's message to the séance participants was anything but. Wicked men, Madini warned, were conspiring against Dee and would stop at nothing to ensure that the queen be stripped of her most loyal confidante. Alarmed, Dee hurriedly packed his belongings, collected his wife and children, and headed eastward along with Kelley and Laski. Dee, by the looks of it, was wise to heed Madini's exhortations. A few weeks later, a gang of thieves jimmied their way into Mortlake manor, looted a number of personal valuables, and turned Dee's prized library upside down.

The threesome arrived at the village of Brill in Buckinghamshire on July 30, where they made a quick stop before proceeding onward to Holland, and later the town of Lubeck in Friesland. They remained in Friesland for a few weeks to rest before setting off once again to Poland. They arrived in the Polish city of Szczecin on Christmas Day and camped out there until mid-January 1584. The temporary exiles only wound up in Laski's home at Lasco in early February.

Once the trio was all settled in, they rolled up their sleeves and went to work on a series of alchemical projects at once. Luckily for Dee and Kelley, the angels were not bound to the former's séance chamber, so they continued to appear whenever called upon. Laski, who was an avid alchemy enthusiast, but was unpracticed in its execution, financed Dee and Kelley's projects, which generally involved transforming iron into gold. Mountains of gold, after all, were required in their quest to remodel the political and societal structure of Europe.

The angels dutifully provided them with a variety of recipes, incantations, and endless tips, but the alchemists met with one failure after another. When it became clear that Laski's treasury had been exhausted, Kelley, predictably, insisted upon severing ties with their Polish patron. Madini and Uriel, Kelley claimed, voiced their misgivings about Laski, and eventually concluded that he was not one of the chosen ones after all.

The three remained together until the end of July, but tensions were rapidly rising. Laski paid closer attention to the progressively distant and taciturn attitudes of both the angels and his alchemists, and after some soul-searching he surmised that he may have ensnared himself in the trap of veteran fraudsters. Holding onto his reservations, Laski allowed them one final test. He scrounged up the funds to sponsor a trip to Prague and arranged a meeting with Emperor Rudolf II. Dee and Kelley pounced on the opportunity, and perhaps not surprisingly, just moments before they were due to depart, the angels called upon Kelley and recited an important message that he was deliver to the emperor.

Rudolf II

    Dee and Kelley were cordially welcomed as honorable guests at Prague, regaled with lavish banquets and chalices brimming with fine wine. Emperor Rudolf II, like many who encountered the pair, was captivated by their unconventional, yet arresting ideas and their relentless ambition. That being said, while Rudolph was prepared to indulge them in their quest for the Philosopher's Stone, he made it no secret that he favored Dee over Kelley because Kelley struck him as unprincipled and full of ulterior motives.

    Even so, Rudolf II allowed the pair to remain in Prague for several months, where they conducted more alchemical experiments and embarked on trips and voyages in pursuit of the stone in the hopes of securing a contract with the emperor. Their projects, regrettably, were cut short on May 22, 1586, when their associate Francesco Pucci notified them that a papal legate was preparing to charge Kelley with the crime of necromancy. In the week that followed, Pope Sixtus V reprimanded Rudolph for condoning this black magic. The complaint Rudolf received must have been something significant, because the emperor swiftly drew up an edict of expulsion and imposed the decree on the pair on the 29th of May.

Pope Sixtus V

Confronted with the ultimatum of leaving within 24 hours or being sentenced to prison or the stake, Dee and Kelley gathered their belongings and headed for Erfurt, Germany. From Erfurt, they traveled to Cassel, but when they failed to spark sufficient interest in their endeavors there, they returned to Krakow. Now that the pair had parted ways with Laski, they had no choice but to support themselves through menial, one-time events, mainly short fortune telling sessions, for the first few weeks.

In time, Dee and Kelley managed to arrange a meeting with the Polish king, Stephen Bathory, whereupon they delivered a message from the angels: Emperor Rudolf II would soon die, leaving his throne vacant for the power-hungry Polish monarch. Just like that, Bathory was hooked and agreed to be a patron for the pair for the rest of the year. But when the alchemists persistently solicited him for more money, all the while producing meager results at best, Bathory began to suspect that he was being strung along.

Bathory was never given the chance to formally discontinue their partnership, as he suddenly died of unknown causes on December 12, 1586. Bathory most likely died as a result of the host of illnesses that plagued him throughout his life, but the rumors flowed. Those in Bathory's court theorized that his demise was a punishment from God, who disapproved of his fraternization with ungodly sorcerers. Other speculators wondered if the monarch's death had been brought about by Dee and Kelley when they learned of Bathory's intentions.

Bathory

Dee became increasingly distressed about their lack of progress, which widened the growing rift between the pair. Kelley was becoming more of a contrarian by the day and began to speak ill of the angel, second-guessing their motives. Dee, on the other hand, wished to resume their contact with the angels, and in his desperation he resorted to inducements and threats in a bid to prolong their partnership.

On April 18, 1587, Kelley once more intimated his decision to step down as Dee's personal scryer. Unwilling to abandon years of hard work, Dee pleaded with him to consult the angels for their advice before settling upon such a rash resolution. Kelley complied, and conveniently, later that day, Madini appeared before Kelley, carrying with her a message so immorally outlandish that the scryer declined to relay it. Dee, of course, was tantalized by Kelley's reaction, and after some persuasion, he convinced his partner to spill the beans. Madini, who supposedly appeared as a fully-grown, beautiful maiden, had shed her clothes in front of Kelley and demanded that the pair "share all things in common," including their wives.

Dee was repulsed by the notion, but his unwavering faith compelled him to apprise Jane of the new arrangement that had been assigned to them. Naturally, Jane, who despised Kelley, shrieked, sobbed, and protested, and she begged her husband to reconsider. Dee himself was torn, even more so when the partners summoned Uriel, who reiterated Madini's command. At last, he acquiesced, chalking the baffling order to a divine test of his faith, and the four parties signed off on a contract drawn on the 3rd of May. "Behold," Madini proclaimed shortly after the ink of their quills seeped into the parchment. "You are now free." It is unclear whether Dee's son, Theodore, who arrived nine months later, was fathered by Kelley.

The toxic collaboration trickled on for the rest of 1587, but the relationship between them was clearly strained. When the Apocalypse failed to transpire the following year, the partnership finally dissolved. Dee applied for and was granted permission to retire to England. Kelley, now a free agent, roamed aimlessly throughout Bohemia peddling his magical snake oil, before returning to the court of Emperor Rudolf II with a new foolproof formula that was guaranteed to transmute iron into gold. Again, Kelley failed to deliver on his promises, and this time he was tossed behind bars. The crafty prisoner succeeded in slithering out of his prison window in February 1598, but he lost his balance and broke his neck in the ensuing fall.

Dee's Final Years

Dee was disheartened by his failures abroad, but at the same time, he was relieved to be able to once again immerse himself in familiar surroundings. His brother-in-law, Nicholas Fromond, had been entrusted with the maintenance and care of his Mortlake estate, but much to Dee's displeasure, Fromond proved himself to be a careless and negligent house-sitter. He failed to properly vet the guests who milled in and out of Dee's private library, which resulted in dozens of thefts. Dee returned to find almost half of his cherished book collection missing. In the years that followed, Dee managed to retrieve a few of his manuscripts, many of which were found to be in the possession of the Marquess of Dorchester, as well as his prized sea compass, but his library was a pitiful cry from the unparalleled treasury it once was. Dee's library steadily dwindled in his final years, to the point that after his death, only about 100 texts remained of the 4,000 manuscripts once housed in the Mortlake manor.

Moreover, Dee's absence, which lasted nearly six years, prevented him from defending himself against the poisonous rumors that swirled around his name. Indeed, the allegations had taken on lives of their own during his leave. In 1594, the disgraced polymath locked himself in his study for days on end and wrote a lengthy, somewhat verbose letter addressed to the Archbishop of Canterbury that was published the following year. The purpose of the letter, entitled "A Letter, Containing a Most Brief Discourse Apologetical," was to "stop the mouths, and at length, to stay the impudent attempts of the rash and malicious deuisers, and contrivers of most untrue, foolish, and wicked reports, and fables of and concerning [his] foresaid studious exercises." The letter emphasized the "great (yea, incredible) pains, travels, cares, and costs" Dee had endured "in the search and learning of true philosophy." Dee also made a point to insert an exhaustive list of the treatises and books he had composed over the years as a testament to his solid character and good intentions.

Sadly, the rumors he so hoped to stamp out continued to linger on. Dee continued to carry out alchemical and chemical experiments, and he soldiered on with his fruitless hunt for the philosopher's stone, but it was clear that the unabating bad press and lackluster results had taken a toll on his drive. Fortune, it appeared, had turned its back on him. Still clinging to the hope of completing his Enochian projects, he hired two scryers, surnamed Bartholomew and Heckman, with what little money he had left. Both scryers failed to summon even a single angel with his "great crystalline globe."

By then, Dee was nearly destitute, but he was thrown a lifeline when Queen Elizabeth I secured him a post as chancellor at St. Paul's Cathedral. A year later, he was granted the wardenship of Christ's College in Manchester. A few months into his tenure, Dee was summoned to investigate the alleged possession of seven local children, whose bodies were inhabited by abominable demonic spirits. Dee, however, had sunk deeper into his depression and failed to conjure up the motivation to tackle the case. Be that as it may, Dee allowed the parents and exorcists to rifle through his collection and kindly lent them the literature they needed. Dee held this post at Christ's College until 1602, when his failing health forced him to tender his resignation.

On March 24, 1603, Queen Elizabeth I, one of the few who remained loyal to Dee, died from sepsis, which only worsened his crippling depression. The throne was filled by the Scottish King James VI, who was thenceforth known as King James I of England. On June 5, 1604, Dee made a final attempt at vindication when he appealed to the new king to grant him royal protection from the slander that continued to soil his name, and he petitioned to be put on trial to free himself of these accusations once and for all. He wrote the king, "[None of the] very strange and frivolous fables or histories reported and told of him were true." Ultimately, the polymath suffered yet another disappointment when his proposal was spurned by King James I, who made his reputation based on his hatred of the occult and his infamous witch trials. That being said, the monarch, while unwilling to help repair Dee's fast-crumbling reputation, showed some mercy by sparing Dee from prison and the stake.

King James I

   By then, Dee, branded an outcast by the court and masses, was in shambles, and the curse of misfortune that had been inflicted upon the miserable man and his family continued to take its course. His son, Michael, died suddenly in 1594 on Dee's birthday, and his other son died in Manchester in 1601. A year after Queen Elizabeth's demise, the bubonic plague, which many ascribed to Dee's black magic, robbed him of his darling wife, and his youngest daughters, Madinia, Margaret, and Frances, are also presumed to have fallen victim to the dreadful pestilence in later years. His sons Arthur and Rowland, as well as his daughter Katherine, were the only ones to outlive their parents. Little else is known about his surviving children because the inconsolable Dee had lost all interest in the upkeep of his diary.

   Dee spent the last years of his life wallowing in his depression, which was further worsened by his indigence and tattered reputation. He cast astrological charts here and there for the few who were unaffected by his bad reputation, but he was forced to lower his rates, raking in little for his services. His penury also left him with no other alternative but to pawn off some of his most treasured books.

John Dee was a broken man when he died at the age of 81 in December 1608. He was in the midst of planning a trip to Germany, which some suggest had been directed by the archangel Raphael. He was subsequently buried near the altar of Mortlake Church.

About a decade after Dee's death, a local antiques dealer by the name of Robert Cotton acquired the Mortlake estate and proceeded to forage through the clutter for valuable documents, manuscripts, and other personal items of note. Cotton hit the jackpot when he unearthed stacks of the records Dee kept of the angelic seances, which he then sold to a French-English scholar named Meric Casaubon. Casaubon, who regarded Dee as a foolish and misguided practitioner of black magic, but recognized the deceased's celebrity, published a compilation of the angelic communications. Entitled *A True and Faithful Relation of What Passed For Many Years Between Dr. John Dee (A Mathematician of Great Fame in Queen Elizabeth and King James Their Reigns) and Some Spirits*, it was released in 1659.

Attached to the compilation was a blistering profile of the alleged necromancer in question. Casaubon described Dee as an unknowing puppet of wicked spirits, one who truly believed he had made contact with the angels, but was, in actuality, conversing with demons. Casaubon's book became a bestseller in just a matter of weeks, and the work is now believed to have molded the public's perception of Dee as a delusional, but ultimately well-meaning crank.

Over 400 years later, people continue to debate whether Dee was a villainous impostor who knowingly scammed royals, nobles, and regular folk alike or a guileless, misunderstood dupe blinded by his own unrealistic ambitions. Either way, his pursuits and reputation have ensured that his name remains well known.

Online Resources

Other books about British history by Charles River Editors

Other books about John Dee by Charles River Editors

Further Reading

Ball, P. (2016, February 24). The maddeningly magical maths of John Dee. Retrieved November 6, 2019, from https://www.newscientist.com/article/2078295-the-maddeningly-magical-maths-of-john-dee/.

Bilyeau, N. (2013, June 16). Conversations with Angels: The Strange Life of Edward Kelley. Retrieved November 6, 2019, from https://englishhistoryauthors.blogspot.com/2013/06/conversations-with-angels-life-of.html.

Calder, I. R. (1952). THE LEGEND OF JOHN DEE. Retrieved November 6, 2019, from http://www.johndee.org/calder/pdf/Calder2.pdf.

Dee, J. (2003). *John Dee's Five Books of Mystery: Original Sourcebook of Enochian Magic.* (J. H. Peterson, Ed.). Weiser Books.

Editors, A. P. (2015, July 8). Ancient Secrets Of John Dee And The Enochian Apocalypse Examined. Retrieved November 6, 2019, from http://www.ancientpages.com/2015/07/08/ancient-secrets-john-dee-enochian-apocalypse-examined/.

Editors, A. B. (2015, January 15). 15 January 1559 – Elizabeth I's coronation and the choice of date. Retrieved November 6, 2019, from https://www.theanneboleynfiles.com/15-january-1559-elizabeth-coronation-choice-date/.

Editors, B. B. (2015, February 19). John Dee was the 16th century's real-life Gandalf. Retrieved November 6, 2019, from https://boingboing.net/2015/02/19/john-dee-was-the-real-life-mer.html.

Editors, B. P. (2015). Mary I. Retrieved November 6, 2019, from https://www.britpolitics.co.uk/queen-mary-i-england-tudor-religion-rebellion/.

Editors, B. E. (2017). John Dee: Astrologer to the Queen. Retrieved November 6, 2019, from https://www.bibliotecapleyades.net/bb/john_dee.htm.

Editors, B. L. (2018). John Dee's spirit mirror. Retrieved November 6, 2019, from https://www.bl.uk/collection-items/john-dees-spirit-mirror.

Editors, B. L. (2018). John Dee's De Heptarchia Mystica, a guide to summoning angels, 1582. Retrieved November 6, 2019, from https://www.bl.uk/collection-items/john-dees-de-heptarchia-mystica-a-guide-to-summoning-angels-1582.

Editors, D. R. (2017). John Dee. Retrieved November 6, 2019, from https://www.deliriumsrealm.com/john-dee/.

Editors, E. (2019, October 18). Dee, John (1527-1608). Retrieved November 6, 2019, from https://www.encyclopedia.com/people/philosophy-and-religion/other-religious-beliefs-biographies/john-dee.

Editors, E. (2019, November 7). Henricus Cornelius Agrippa. Retrieved November 6, 2019, from https://www.encyclopedia.com/people/philosophy-and-religion/other-religious-beliefs-biographies/henricus-cornelius-agrippa.

Editors, F. (2014). 42 Mystical Facts About John Dee, The Queen's Dark Conjurer. Retrieved November 6, 2019, from https://www.factinate.com/people/facts-john-dee/.

Editors, H. A. (2013, April 25). Paracelsus. Retrieved November 6, 2019, from http://historyofalchemy.com/list-of-alchemists/paracelsus/.

Editors, N. W. (2018, May 15). John Dee. Retrieved November 6, 2019, from https://www.newworldencyclopedia.org/entry/John_Dee#Early_professional_life.

Editors, O. P. (2017). Dee, John (1527-1608). Retrieved November 6, 2019, from http://www.occultopedia.com/d/dee.htm.

Editors, O. (2018). Crystalomancy. Retrieved November 6, 2019, from http://www.occultopedia.com/c/crystalomancy.htm.

Editors, S. A. (2016). John Dee – A Timeline. Retrieved November 6, 2019, from https://solascendans.com/articles/dee/.

Editors, T. D. (2011, March 31). UNEARTHLY TERRITORY: THE ENIGMA THAT WAS JOHN DEE. Retrieved November 6, 2019, from https://taboodada.wordpress.com/2011/03/31/unearthly-territory-the-enigma-that-was-john-dee/.

Editors, U. A. (2002, August). John Dee. Retrieved November 6, 2019, from http://www-history.mcs.st-and.ac.uk/Biographies/Dee.html.

Editors, W. O. (2016, July 20). The Story Of Dr. John Dee. Retrieved November 6, 2019, from https://wolfofantimonyoccultism.tumblr.com/post/147719877246/the-story-of-dr-john-dee.

Editors, W. (2019, October 14). John Dee. Retrieved November 6, 2AD, from https://en.wikipedia.org/wiki/John_Dee.

French, P. J. (2013). *John Dee: The World of the Elizabethan Magus*. Routledge.

Gentle, P. (2002). Dr. John Dee - The Original 007. Retrieved November 6, 2019, from http://www.woe.edu.pl/content/dr-john-dee-original-007.

Hall, E., & Wrigley, A. (2007). *Aristophanes in Performance, 421 Bc-Ad 2007: Peace, Birds and Frogs*. MHRA.

Halliwell, J. O. (Ed.). (2016, October 16). The Private Diary of Dr. John Dee And the Catalog of His Library of Manuscripts. Retrieved November 6, 2019, from http://www.gutenberg.org/files/19553/19553-h/19553-h.htm.

Hill, B. (2019, June 8). Enochian: The Mysterious Lost Language of Angels. Retrieved November 6, 2019, from https://www.ancient-origins.net/artifacts-ancient-writings/enochian-mysterious-lost-language-angels-003100.

Hort, R. B. (1993). *Three Famous Occultists: Dr. John Dee, Franz Anton Mesmer and Thomas Lake Harris*. Health Research Books.

Håkansson, H. (2001). Seeing the Word : John Dee and Renaissance Occultism. Retrieved November 6, 2019, from https://portal.research.lu.se/ws/files/4651687/3402822.pdf.

Ingham, A. (2016, November 26). Lady Jane Grey Is Deposed by Mary I of England. Retrieved November 6, 2019, from https://owlcation.com/humanities/Lady-Jane-Grey-Is-Deposed-by-Mary-I-of-England.

Johnson, S. R. (2016). CHEKE, John (1514-57), of Cambridge and London. Retrieved November 6, 2019, from http://www.histparl.ac.uk/volume/1509-1558/member/cheke-john-1514-57.

Klimczak, N. (2016, May 22). Following the Magical Journey to Poland by John Dee and Edward Kelley. Retrieved November 6, 2019, from https://www.ancient-origins.net/history-famous-people/following-magical-journey-poland-john-dee-and-edward-kelley-005945.

Lewis, B. R. (2006, June 12). Was Mary Tudor Really England's Most Hated Queen? Retrieved November 6, 2019, from https://britishheritage.com/royals/who-is-mary-tudor.

Loades, D. (2017). Why Queen Mary Was Bloody. Retrieved November 6, 2019, from https://www.christianitytoday.com/history/issues/issue-48/why-queen-mary-was-bloody.html.

Louv, J. (2018). *John Dee and the Empire of Angels: Enochian Magick and the Occult Roots of the Modern World*. Simon and Schuster.

Maranzani, B. (2018, August 22). What's so unlucky about the number 13? Retrieved November 6, 2019, from https://www.history.com/news/whats-so-unlucky-about-the-number-13.

Martin, T. (2016, January 10). John Dee: the man who spoke to angels. Retrieved November 6, 2AD, from https://www.telegraph.co.uk/books/authors/the-man-who-spoke-to-angels/.

Matthew, A. (2019). A JOHN DEE CHRONOLOGY, 1509-1609. Retrieved November 6, 2019, from http://www.ampltd.co.uk/digital_guides/ren_man_series1_prt1/chronology.aspx.

Mcilvenna, U. (2018, October 25). What Inspired Queen 'Bloody' Mary's Gruesome Nickname? Retrieved November 6, 2019, from https://www.history.com/news/queen-mary-i-bloody-mary-reformation.

Moss, R. (2015, January 14). New John Dee discovery reveals resemblance to mother and a mysterious 'dwarf'. Retrieved November 6, 2019, from https://www.culture24.org.uk/history-

and-heritage/royal-history/art544763-new-john-dee-discovery-reveals-resemblance-to-mother-and-a-mysterious-dwarf.

Mudhar, R. (2017, March 23). John Dee, Queen Elizabeth I Astronomer-Royal's magickal scrying mirror in the British Museum. Retrieved November 6, 2019, from https://www.richardmudhar.com/blog/tag/shew-stone/.

Palisca, C. V. (2001, January). Gogava, Antonius Hermannus. Retrieved November 6, 2019, from https://oxfordindex.oup.com/view/10.1093/gmo/9781561592630.article.11364.

Peterson, J. H. (1999). A LETTER. Retrieved November 6, 2019, from http://www.esotericarchives.com/dee/aletter.htm.

Peterson, J. H. (2019, May 29). Heinrich Cornelius Agrippa: Of Occult Philosophy, Book I. (part 1). Retrieved November 6, 2019, from http://www.esotericarchives.com/agrippa/agrippa1.htm.

Rampling, J. M. (2012, September). John Dee and the sciences: early modern networks of knowledge. Retrieved November 6, 2019, from https://www.ncbi.nlm.nih.gov/pmc/articles/PMC3778877/.

Rimmer, J. (2008). Life of Dr Dee. Retrieved November 6, 2019, from http://jdoms.blogspot.com/p/john-dee-was-born-in-city-of-london.html.

Rounding, V. (2017). *The Burning Time: The Story of the Smithfield Martyrs*. Pan Macmillan.

Rutledge, L. A. (2011, November 29). John Dee: Consultant to Queen Elizabeth I . Retrieved November 6, 2019, from https://www.nsa.gov/Portals/70/documents/news-features/declassified-documents/tech-journals/john-dee.pdf.

Sangha, L. (2012, November 9). John Dee's conversations with Angels. Retrieved November 6, 2019, from https://manyheadedmonster.wordpress.com/2012/11/09/john-dees-conversations-with-angels/.

Teth, A. (2017). Enochian Introduction. Retrieved November 6, 2019, from http://anthonyteth.com/enochian-introduction/.

Wigington, P. (2019, July 11). Biography of John Dee. Retrieved November 6, 2019, from https://www.thoughtco.com/john-dee-biography-4158012.

Winscher, S. (2016, September 5). "King James and the Era of the Witch Trials." Retrieved November 6, 2019, from https://ahr-ashford.com/king-james-and-the-era-of-the-witch-trials/.

Free Books by Charles River Editors

We have brand new titles available for free most days of the week. To see which of our titles are currently free, click on this link.

Discounted Books by Charles River Editors

We have titles at a discount price of just 99 cents everyday. To see which of our titles are currently 99 cents, click on this link.

Printed in Dunstable, United Kingdom